CASTING
OUT
DEMONS

D1040496

CASTING OUT DEMONS

H.A.
MAXWELL
WHYTE

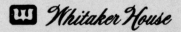 Whitaker House

Unless otherwise indicated, all Scripture quotations are taken from the King James Version (KJV) of the Holy Bible.

CASTING OUT DEMONS
(previously published as *Dominion over Demons*)

ISBN: 0-88368-468-3
Printed in the United States of America
© 1973 by Banner Publishing, a division of Whitaker House

Whitaker House
30 Hunt Valley Circle
New Kensington, PA 15068
web site: www.whitakerhouse.com

4 5 6 7 8 9 10 11 12 / 09 08 07 06 05 04 03 02

FOREWORD

I first met Pastor H. A. Maxwell Whyte nearly a decade ago, while I was minister of a church in Toronto, Canada, the city where he has also pastored for many years. At the time I was not involved in a charismatic ministry and found myself almost critical of his deep spiritual convictions.

"That man sounds too sure of himself," I told myself. In those days I had no awareness or understanding of Maxwell Whyte's powerful ministry.

But in subsequent years the Holy Spirit began to reveal to me the reality of the spiritual warfare we are engaged in, and to show me the necessity of exercising the authority given us in the name of Jesus Christ over the powers of darkness.

As I found myself being drawn into the strange

and dramatic ministry of deliverance, a number of Maxwell Whyte's booklets came into my possession—proving a source of real inspiration, information and encouragement. I was delighted therefore, when Banner Publishing (publisher of a number of my own writings) informed me of their plans to publish an enlarged edition of *Casting Out Demons,* requesting that I write a brief introduction.

In this day of dramatic return to miraculous ministries in the Body of Christ, we must look to those who have not only the gifts, but also the fruit of Christ's ministry in their lives. H. A. Maxwell Whyte is such a man. Not only is his teaching ministry widely recognized across all North America, but for over twenty years he has also maintained a respected and effectual pastoral ministry in his own city of Toronto.

This unique combination of traveling apostle and effective pastor is eloquent testimony to the validity of his ministry.

I personally owe a debt of gratitude to Maxwell Whyte for the influence he had in the development of my own ministry. I have had the privilege of ministering with him in charismatic seminars in various cities and have spoken from his own pulpit. I recognize him as a true servant of God, powerful in ministry, learned in the

Scriptures and uncompromising in his convictions. He is also a close personal friend.

It is therefore a privilege to commend this latest publication of his to every Christian who longs to unleash the Spirit's power in his life.

Don W. Basham

CONTENTS

PREFACE

In the beginning of this ministry in 1948, it was normal to spend from one half to 2 hours in prayer for the oppressed; this became very exhausting and demanding on my time and strength. Over the years I began to see that this deliverance ministry could and should be speeded up, and that it depended on two factors: our own understanding of our tremendous authority in Christ, and the willing collaboration and sympathy of the one being delivered.

We began to tell Satan that he was not going to temporize or stall, and we commanded him to come out *immediately*, and he began to do so. Deliverances which might have taken an hour now took 2 or 3 minutes, and we could pray in line for many, one after another, and evil spirits

would come out coughing, choking and screaming. Many people fell to the ground as the process was completed, and then rose to their feet
praising God, FREE!

I refused to talk to demons any more, nor did
I encourage them to speak, or confess their names
or presence; the Holy Spirit showed me all I
needed to know. Jesus commanded them to hold
their peace and come out; this seemed to be the
pattern. We did the same and they obeyed. We
learned that if we were uncertain, Satan and his
demons took advantage of us, and put on a show
and demonstration, either refusing to come out,
or coming out only very slowly while we fought.

Every week in our church in Scarborough, a
suburb of Toronto, Ontario, many come for release and the infilling of the Spirit; it is almost
impossible to catalogue the different cases, nor
do we try. We "process" those who come. Arthritis, heart troubles, lung troubles, throat troubles, jealousy, anger, hatred, self pity, murder,
suicide, smoking, drinking, unlawful sex, and
drugs. People with such problems come in a
steady stream to us, and God, through our pray-
ers, brings permanent deliverance to most of
them. Immediately after their manifest deliverance, we ask them if they would like the Holy
Spirit to come in and fill all the areas previously

occupied by alien spirits. They agree, whether they understand much or not, for they are hungry, and in many cases, they start to speak in tongues as the Holy Spirit comes in (much to their astonishment). What a change on their faces!

Countless thousands need this ministry in our churches today. It is pointless to argue whether they are "saved" or not. They need help in whatever spiritual condition they may be, and God has come down to deliver today as He did in Moses' day. He is raising up a ministry today where people are having their needs met.

REV. H. A. MAXWELL WHYTE

CHAPTER 1

THE STRANGE WORLD OF SPIRITS

"You foul spirit of fear, come out of her in Jesus Name!" I commanded. I knew that nothing else would help her.

It was in the closing moments of a home prayer meeting in Florida. A few people had decided to stay for the prayer of deliverance. Among these was this fearful woman, who had also been troubled with a stiff neck for many years.

I began to pray, as in all such cases, by commanding the spirit of fear to come out of her. Immediately there was a reaction, and for the next few minutes this spirit began to choke out of her, until peace returned.

Then God brought to her mind the following

explanation of how she had come to be in this miserable condition in the first place. When she was five years of age, it had been customary for her father to tell her bedtime stories. These were not edifying stories, but terrifying ones. One night he outdid himself in horror fiction. The hero of the story was "Mr. Bloodybones, the Ghost." The details were so frightening that the child began to scream in terror. The mother came in and commanded her well-meaning husband to get out of the room. She then tried to speak pacifying words to her child, but it was too late; the damage had been done.

When her mother went out of the room, the little girl buried herself underneath a patchwork quilt, completely petrified with fear at the memory of her Daddy's gruesome story.

Finally, as a result of this terrifying experience, a spirit of fear entered her, remaining for 50 years and bringing with it a spirit of tension, causing stiffness in the neck. So you can imagine how relieved she was when we cast that demon out of her.

I am well aware that this kind of ministry is difficult for some to understand. So, at the outset, let me open the Bible and introduce you to this teaching about the strange world of spirits.

In I Thessalonians 5:23, you will read the prayer of the Apostle Paul that "your whole spirit and soul and body be preserved blameless unto the coming of our Lord Jesus Christ." Man is triune.

16

First spirit. Then soul. Then body. Man is, therefore, primarily and essentially a spiritual being.

Way back in the beginning, God fashioned a human body out of the dust of this earth, and then breathed into this lifeless body the breath of life. I do not believe that God merely expanded Adam's lungs with fresh air. Obviously, it would take more than this to cause him to live. I believe that God literally breathed into man His own life. He breathed *spirit* into him, for God *is* Spirit.

Man is, therefore, first a spiritual being. He was never intended to use his mind apart from his spirit. This is a great problem in the world today, for our modern educational systems are designed on the level of the mind. The mind of man teaches the mind of man, but the spirit of man is completely ignored. In fact, unregenerate men simply do not grasp the spiritual needs of man at all. As the Scriptures say, "The natural man receiveth not the things of the Spirit of God: for they are foolishness unto him: neither can he know them, because they are spiritually discerned" (I Corinthians 2:14).

The mind can understand only the things of the mind, and likewise the spirit the things of the Spirit. An old adage states that "Birds of a feather flock together." Like always goes with like. A church which ministers to the needs of the human spirit will draw in spiritual people. But most religion simply manifests excess of fleshly feeling. The body, with its five senses of touch, taste, smell, hearing and seeing, likes to be petted and allowed to produce a substitute for true spiritual worship of God in the Spirit. But Jesus said that God is looking for those who will worship Him "in *spirit* and in truth" (John 4:23).

We cannot worship God with our minds or intellects, for this is soulish religion. Long ago Job wrote, "Canst thou by searching find out God?" The answer is *No*. We cannot find God or understand anything about God with our minds or our bodies. Therefore, God made man a spiritual being.

Like goes to like. "Deep calleth unto deep." If man wishes to find out God, then the Creator has so made him that he may do so through his spirit. If we desire to listen to a radio program, it is necessary that we tune the frequency of our receiver to exactly the same frequency as that of the transmitter. In this way, we can get perfect reception if we are in range. In like manner, Almighty God is a Spirit; and the spiritual part of our triune nature can communicate with Him when we are tuned in through the working of the Holy Spirit.

When we commune with God, we do so with our spirits; then only do we begin to understand the mind of God. We begin to realize that God gives us some of His mind (I Corinthians 2:16). We begin to think as God thinks, but only in part, of course. Our minds become actuated by our regenerated spirit in communion with God.

This actuating of the mind becomes greatly

quickened within us when we are baptized in the Holy Spirit. We then begin to understand how God imparts such gifts as a word of wisdom and knowledge, discerning of spirits, tongues, interpretation and prophecy. These come from the Spirit of God through the human spirit, not through the mind.

If they came through our minds, then it could be said that "we just thought them up." But since they come down from God, we do not think them up at all; we simply receive them through our spirits. Any so-called gift which comes only from the human mind is a counterfeit gift.

On either side of the spirit of man are two spiritual powers calling for his attention. On the one hand is God and the angels who kept their first estate (Hebrews 1:7), i.e., the angels who never sinned. On the other hand is Satan, who left his state of perfection to become the devil. Many believe that he took with him one-third of all the created angelic beings, and that these now constitute the demons that torment and afflict all mankind. Lucifer and God's angels became Satan and his demons.

Once a man is born again and learns the secret of using his spirit instead of his mind, he has opened the door into the spiritual realm. It is now possible for him to have communication with other spiritual beings. And this is spiritual dynamite. By the operation of his own free will, he can have free converse with Almighty God and with the angels from time to time. But unless he maintains his integrity and his righteous standing before God, he can easily be seduced by an angel of light (I Timothy 4:1; II Corinthians 11:13–15), who will come to woo him in much the same way as an immoral woman would endeavor to win the affections of a married man.

It is a sad state of affairs today that so many Christians who attend church regularly are being deceived by these angels of light, and are sources of grave troubles to their patient pastor, who is trying to teach by God's Spirit. No wonder Jesus said we need to be as wise as serpents, and harmless as doves (Matthew 10:16). We need to be one step ahead of Satan all of the time, so that his beautiful seducing spirits do not come and pretend to be the Holy Spirit, and thus deceive us.

A good illustration of the work of an angel of light is recorded in Acts 16, where a young girl followed Paul and Silas crying, "These men are the servants of the most high God, which show unto us the way of salvation." What she said was true, and many in our Full Gospel churches today would have applauded such an utterance as being of the Holy Spirit. But Paul was grieved, and turned *to the spirit* and said, "I command thee in the Name of Jesus Christ to come out of her. And he came out the same hour."

This raises the question, "How do we know whether we are communicating with the Holy

Spirit or with an evil spirit then?" The answer to this question is found in I John 4:1: "Beloved, believe not every spirit, but try the spirits whether they are of God: because many false prophets are gone out into the world." Then John goes on to give some specific instructions about how to go about trying the spirits: "Hereby know ye the Spirit of God: Every spirit that confesseth that Jesus Christ is come in the flesh is of God; And every spirit that confesseth not that Jesus Christ is come in the flesh is not of God: and this is that spirit of antichrist, whereof ye have heard that it should come; and even now already is it in the world."

Again, we are reminded of the words of Jesus in Matthew 24: "For there shall arise false Christs, and false prophets, and shall show great signs and wonders; insomuch that, if it were possible, they shall deceive the very elect." In the current revival of the supernatural, we need to be very careful to check every miracle with the Word of God.

If we do not do this, we are likely to be easily deceived. A sign or a wonder does not of necessity have to be of God. It can be of Satan. The blood of Jesus Christ is still our greatest safeguard. And we would urge that the blood be used in faith to test all that we receive from the world of spirits. Evil spirits are greatly agitated at the mention of the blood of Jesus. We should practice the pleading of the blood of Jesus much more than we do.

Besides this, God has put into the church a gift of discerning spirits, and I do not believe that He intended this gift to be used by the pastor only. This gift is for all children of God, although the pastor is sent by the Holy Spirit to administer the things of the Spirit to the people.

A case in point happened in Erie, Pennsylvania, at a convention where I was speaking. A man stood up and shouted that a certain evangelist was a man of God, and that the people should give heed to him. This he did three times, disturbing the meeting. Several men endeavored to quiet him, but this was a demon, not the spirit of the man. I arose from my seat, discerning the evil spirit, and commanded it to be silent in the Name of Jesus. No further trouble was experienced from this man.

So, you see, it is highly important for the protection of the Church that we know how to discern evil spirits, and how to deal with them.

CHAPTER 2

THE BLOOD LINE

The startling fact of the Satanic oppression of certain Christians was vividly demonstrated one hot August day in Huntingdon Beach, California. I was speaking to a charismatic group in a restaurant, and it was full. I told of the ministry of Jesus in healing the sick and casting out demons, and explained that He was willing to do the same things for us today. After the preaching, I began to pray for people with various needs, and many coughed, choked and showed the usual manifestations of deliverance that happen each time I minister.

One man had a locked spine. He could not bend himself, and said he had been this way for 20 years. He could walk upright, but not bend, for his spine was "frozen."

I explained to him that this was probably caused by a spirit of infirmity, and reminded him of the lady in the Bible who had a similar condition:

> *"And, behold, there was a woman which had a spirit of infirmity eighteen years, and was bowed together, and could in no wise lift up herself. And when Jesus saw her, he called her to him, and said unto her, Woman, thou art loosed from thine infirmity. And he laid his hands on her: and immediately she was straight, and glorified God."*
>
> Luke 13:11–13

I emphasized the fact that the woman's condition was caused by a demon—by a "spirit of infirmity." I then laid hands on the man before me and rebuked the spirit of infirmity, and commanded it to come out of his spine.

"Now, 'I said to the man,' just start bending your back, and keep on bending until you can touch your toes."

He looked at me somewhat startled. "I have not been able to do that for 20 years!"

But he began bending, and slowly but surely, each time he bent down, he got closer to his toes. After eight minutes he started to shout. He had touched his toes! Twenty years of crippling had gone in eight minutes!

We have heard some people get really upset when we tell them that Satan may deceive them or visit sickness on them, or cause them to backslide, or seduce them. They reply that "Satan cannot get through the Blood line," which is a teaching frequently expounded by some evangelists. Of course, I agree that Satan cannot get through the Blood line if it is there! It is not automatic!

Long ago, Job had a nice, snug hedge around him. Satan used to prowl around this hedge day and night waiting for a hole to appear. And one day a hole *did* appear, created by Job himself because he started to be afraid. Job's fear had torn down God's defences. Remember what Job said? "The thing which I *greatly feared* is come upon me, and that which I was afraid of is come unto me" (Job 3:25). So you see, *God* had not torn down the hedge. But Job had *created* a hole in the hedge *by his own fear*. The situation is clearly described in Ecclesiastes 10:8: "Whosoever breaketh an hedge, a serpent shall bite him." Job began to be afraid, and God's protection could no longer operate, because faith cannot exist where fear is present. And so the Arch Serpent went in and nearly destroyed Job's life. It is up to every child of God to keep himself consciously covered and washed in the Blood of Jesus Christ every moment of every day. This, I believe, is the secret place of the Most High of Psalm 91.

Man, being essentially a spiritual being, can hear either the voice of the Spirit of God or of Satan and his demon spirits. Many nervous breakdowns have occurred because clean-minded, Holy Ghost-baptized Christians have been greatly disturbed at voices putting evil suggestions into their minds. Others have been known to doubt their salvation, and ultimately lose their minds because of evil mental pictures which Satan has given them, and which they thought they should not think or see.

It must be understood by Christians that the moment we open the door of our spirit to the world of spirits, we can receive whatever voice we tune into. A short-wave radio receiver does not differentiate between Russian stations or American stations; it simply hears what it tunes into. Likewise with the human spirit. But with a radio, we can tune out radio Moscow if we do not like the propaganda, and in like manner we can tune out the unwanted Satanic voices and re-tune into God's frequency. It is an act of the free will.

Pleading the Blood of Jesus causes Satan's voice to be stilled. We have met many Christian people who tell us that Satan told them this and that, or gave them this foul thought or that foul thought. But remember, it is not wrong to hear a Satanic voice. It is wrong to obey it! It is wrong to allow yourself to become obsessed with his voice. People who keep on listening to Satan are rapidly on their way to becoming demon obsessed. We must refuse to believe the lies of the devil and believe the truth of God's Word.

We have met hundreds of dear children of God who tell us that Satan says they are not saved, whereas the Word of God says just the opposite.

Which are we to believe? The Spirit of God bears witness to the Scripture which says we are saved by faith, but Satan says, "Oh no, you are not!" Is not this the age-old stratagem of the devil in the garden of Eden? "Hath God said . . . ?" What a liar he is!

In our presentations on the subject of demonology, we have met blank refusal on the part of thousands of Christians, including Full Gospel people, to believe that Satan can worry, afflict, oppress, suppress, depress, frustrate, speak to or lie to a child of God. These dear people take the unscriptural attitude that once they are a child of God, washed in the Blood of Christ, then Satan can have nothing further to do with them. This teaching is from the pit!

As a natural child has to wash his body daily with soap and water, so do we need the continual cleansing of the Blood of Christ. We do not take the Lord's supper once after conversion, and then never come together to take it again, do we? Then why should we regard the cleansing of the Blood of Christ in this way? We need continual cleansing. It is written that "the blood of Jesus Christ cleanses us from all sin" (I John 1:7). Note that "cleanses" is in the present tense. This means that it *continually* cleanses—not once in the past, but progressively now and in the future.

If Christians cannot be afflicted by Satan and his demons, why then do we read of no less than three admonitions from New Testament writers on this subject? We need to read these admonitions carefully: (1) Paul: "Neither give place to the devil" (Ephesians 4:27). And again (2) Peter: "Be sober, be vigilant; because your adversary the devil, as a roaring lion, walketh about, seeking whom he may devour; Whom resist steadfast in the faith . . ." (I Peter 5:8–9). And again (3) James: "Resist the devil and he will flee from you" (James 4:7). These New Testament apostles were addressing themselves to Holy Ghost-baptized Christians who had opened their lives, minds, and hearts to the Holy Spirit and could therefore expect Satan to try to gain entrance again. It was highly important that they be reminded of this, for the Holy Spirit is likened to a dove, a gentle creature that can easily be frightened away.

The classic case of Satan actually possessing a child of God is that of Judas Iscariot, whom Jesus had chosen as an apostle and disciple. It seems unthinkable that Jesus would have chosen an unsaved man to heal the sick and cast out devils! Obviously, Judas was in the right place once, even as many Christians are today. They begin well.

In John 13:2, we read of how Satan tempted Judas to do his foul deed: "And supper being ended, the devil having now put into the heart of Judas Iscariot . . . to betray him. . . ." The first act of the devil was to speak to Judas and *put the thought into his heart*, the innermost seat of his affections. Judas decided by the operation of his own free will to obey Satan, and therefore turn his back on God and His Word. Judas, the disciple, was first oppressed, but finally he was possessed! In verse 27 of the same chapter we read, "And after the sop, Satan *entered into* him." If Judas Iscariot could end up by being possessed of the devil, how much more can we today? For remember, Satan knows that his time is short, and he is working harder than ever before to break down what God is building in human lives. Simply because you are saved and filled with God's Spirit must not be taken as an automatic guarantee that you will continue so.

Unless we realize these things we will have no understanding of why so many Christians get sick in body, as well as mind. Why is it that so many Christians today are going into mental homes? This is not the fault of the Gospel, for Jesus came to deliver us from the prison house (Luke 4:18). It is because those who have been delivered by faith in Christ begin to listen to the temptations of Satan and fall into his snare, thereby tacitly ignoring God's Word.

We would add that there is nothing automatic about salvation, or about any of the promises of God. These must be embraced in faith continually; we must resist the devil daily. If we do not, it is not God's fault that we break the hedge and the serpent bites us.

CHAPTER 3

THE SNARE OF DECEPTIONS

So many people try to feel something when they seek the Holy Spirit, quite overlooking the fact that feelings come *after* the Holy Spirit comes in. Just because they reeled as drunken men on the day of Pentecost is no reason for us to try to perpetuate a drunken reeling every time we speak in tongues. In understanding be men! (I Corinthians 14:20) Do not trust your feelings, but only the pure Word of God.

It is natural that when a person becomes born again and filled with the Holy Spirit, some intense emotion will be felt. And the degree of emotion will be in proportion to the make-up of the person. A Scot might feel less emotion than a Frenchman, or a Pennsylvania Dutchman less than a Texan.

The baptism in the Spirit is not given to us to perpetuate feelings, but to enable us to fight the devil in faith whether we feel good or not.

Unfortunately Satan has been very clever in diverting thousands of Holy Ghost-baptized Christians into an orgy of feelings and emotions. The Gospel owes nothing to the human emotions; it is all of faith in God's Word. But many sincere Christians do not understand this. When they are manifesting the gift of tongues or prophecy, they feel they must draw attention to themselves by waving their arms, jerking their bodies or using falsetto voices, in order to impress others with the "tremendous anointing of the Spirit" which they feel. All of these fleshly additions are unnecessary, and are caused by the work of a deceiving spirit. The words spoken may be of God, but the manifestation is of the flesh.

I remember casting a religious demon out of a lady who kept on crying "Hallelujah" in an unnaturally high voice. After the demon came out, she collapsed in a heap and couldn't say a word. The church is swarming with religious demons today who are simulating holy things.

On the other hand, there are many sincere Christians who are afraid to speak in tongues lest they get "in the flesh," as they say. They believe that you must feel something before you speak. But you must remember that the use of the gifts of the Spirit is an act of faith. So let us divorce our feelings from faith, and exercise our divine authority whether we feel anything or not.

I remember a convention in Toronto where a man made a great disturbance. Toward the close of the meeting many hundreds swarmed up to the platform to seek the Holy Spirit. This man was continuing to make a nuisance of himself, but many Christians thought that he was under the power of the Spirit. Finally, I could stand his disturbance no longer, and I approached him and commanded the religious demon to come out of him. Immediately, he ceased to disturb anymore. You see, not everything that happens in a Pentecostal meeting is necessarily of the Holy Spirit. Many things that occur are of the *human* spirit which has not been correctly disciplined. And other disturbances are the work of *evil* spirits who have taken control of the person.

Now I realize that many people are shocked at such revelations. If the devil can simulate religious things, then it is entirely possible that speaking in tongues may not necessarily be a sign of the indwelling Holy Spirit! I know this presents a problem in the minds of many people, but the answer, I believe, is simple.

A demon is a created, living being. Long before man was upon the earth, the angelic beings that fell from their high estate in Heaven were cast out to the earth with their leader, Satan (Revelation 12:7–8). Perhaps you can imagine a demon gaining possession of a man in China a thousand years ago. That demon would learn to speak Chinese by indwelling that man. Then try to imagine that same demon having to leave the body of this man at death; he would then seek to indwell another human body, and *this* time he might enter an Indian and learn *his* language. Upon the death of the Indian, he might well live in the human bodies of many men and women of different nationalities. And he would learn all of their languages.

Now, imagine this multi-lingual demon coming into an English-speaking man, who came to one of our Pentecostal churches, nicely dressed and • with good appearance. We would receive him without question, and presently he would raise his hands and we would hear Chinese, Indian, French, Hottentot! Many would say the man had been baptized in the Holy Spirit!

Even in Moses' day the deceptions of the devil were marvelous. Moses confidently threw down his rod at the command of God and it became a serpent; but Jannes and Jambres, the magicians of Pharaoh's court, did exactly the same. Then Moses lifted up his rod again and the waters of Egypt became blood, but Jannes and Jambres did the same! A third time Moses raised his rod and brought forth frogs from the waters, but the magicians also brought up frogs (Exodus 7); it was not until the fourth plague of dust being turned into lice that the magicians could no longer keep pace with God's man and the power of God. People are so gullible today that they will believe any miracle, any sign, any wonder and say it must be of God! Let us be wise as serpents.

We would like to say that whereas Satan can speak in tongues through a person, we must not be afraid to face up to the scriptural fact that everyone truly baptized in the Spirit can also speak in tongues as the Holy Spirit gives the utterance (Acts 2:4). But how may we know the difference? Jesus gives the answer: "By their fruits ye shall know them" (Matthew 7:16). If a tongues-speaking Christian does not manifest the fruit of the Spirit (Galatians 5:22) in his life, he must be suspect in the Assembly.

I believe that a pastor has divinely implanted authority to insist that an unruly member keep silence in the church, less he give an utterance of an evil spirit, or of his own human spirit, instead of the Holy Spirit. And such a thing is altogether possible if a Christian does not walk in close fellowship with God.

This fact throws some light on Matthew 7:22,23, where Jesus says, "Many will say to me in that day, Lord, Lord, have we not prophesied in thy name? and in thy name have cast out devils? and in thy name done many wonderful works? And then will I profess unto them, I never knew you: depart from me, ye that work iniquity." How could these people have cast out devils, and prophesied and done signs and wonders and miracles? Surely, like Judas Iscariot, they must have been in right relationship with God at one time, well received and well beloved in the local assembly. But what happened to them? They gave place to the demon of pride, power, avarice, lust, jealousy, etc., and Jesus had no place for them in His Kingdom. Tongues didn't save them; prophesying didn't save them. "Ye shall know them by their fruits," said Jesus. Paul brings this to our minds clearly in I Corinthians 14:1 where he says that we should seek both the fruits included in the all-embracing fruit of love, as well as the nine gifts of I Corinthians 12:8–10. The gifts without the fruits profit no one, including the user. Fruits without the gifts are beautiful, but lack power. We need nine gifts and nine fruits working in symmetry and harmony in this last-day revival of the supernatural.

CHAPTER 4

SOME PRACTICAL THINGS

It was at the beginning of 1948 that God began to speak to many Christians on the subject of the Gospel of divine deliverance for spirit, soul and body. At this time we had in our Toronto church a fine, converted, Roman Catholic man who was a chronic sufferer from asthma from birth. This man was also a heavy smoker, and although we prayed for him in the assembly and anointed him with oil, he was no better. The asthma still stuck to him stubbornly, and he could not quit smoking.

It was then that a lady suggested to me what, at the time, seemed a preposterous thought. She said, "Do you suppose this is a smoking demon?"

I had never heard of a smoking demon, and many refuse to hear of them today either! If you

had told me that there was an asthma demon too, I
would have found it most hard to believe, because
after all, was not asthma a nervous disease, and
smoking merely a dirty habit? Demon? Devil? Evil
spirit? How could it be? The Spirit of God was
working on me to lead me and teach me many
things I could never have learned in Bible schools!

First, I prayed with this man to receive everything from God, but still he remained bound. He
had developed asthma as a baby and had not been
able to work until he was twenty-six. For the next
fourteen years he spent all of his hard-earned
money on doctor bills, hoping to find a little relief.

I prayed with him, and he was graciously baptized in the Holy Spirit, speaking in tongues and
magnifying God, but still the asthma and smoking
stuck. I am sure many will refuse to believe this,
because they have been taught that the Holy Spirit
will not enter into an unclean vessel, but we were
learning things! The Holy Spirit is given, like every
other gift of God, on the basis of faith, not of our
worthiness or holiness.

One day I said to this brother, "We would like
to carry out an experiment with you. It is possible
that you may have a smoking demon."

He wasn't shocked, for in the Roman church he
had learned to look upon what the priest said as
true. I suppose this is a great lesson for rebellious
Protestants to learn! We took him down into the
church kitchen in the basement, for we had read

37

that demons sometimes come out crying with a loud voice, but of course we had had no first-hand experience in these matters.

My wife and I sat down, and our friend sat in front of us. I knew nothing except what Jesus had told me (and this is always enough!). He had said, "In my Name shall ye cast out devils" (Mark 16:17); in addition I remembered all of the teaching I had received about using the Blood of Jesus in the presence of the destroyer. So, we started to sing some choruses about the Blood never losing its power. Then we attacked! "In the Name of Jesus, come out!" This was kept up, and as we pressed the battle hard, the demons of asthma and smoking started to cough out and vomit out, and after one hour and twenty minutes there was on the floor a huge pile of handkerchiefs soaked with sputum; but he was healed! He stood up and breathed a deep breath down to the bottom of his lungs and exclaimed, "Praise God! I am healed! I can breathe properly for the first time in my life!"

What had we done? We had "wrestled, not with flesh and blood, but with wicked spirits . . ." (Ephesians 6:12). We had cast out "spirits of infirmity." Yes, though asthma is a nervous disease, we had learned that a demon can be the cause of the irritation of the nerves! This brother is still healed today, and his heart was pronounced strong five years after the healing. He is healed and no longer needs to smoke, for Jesus set him free. He still speaks in tongues and interprets and prophesies in the assembly.

We were learning things. It is said that one ounce of experience is worth a ton of theory. Our Bible Schools have been stuffing the heads of students with theory, so that many of them would not recognize a demon if they saw one. And if they suspected that they were seeing a demon, they would run from it! The gift of discerning of spirits is notably absent from the church today!

Two days later, another Christian brother telephoned us. He had been a deacon in a Full Gospel assembly. He was in great trouble, saying he had a strong urge to commit suicide. Could it be that a Holy Ghost-baptized man—a deacon in a Full Gospel assembly—could be demon possessed? What would our Bible Schools say? What would the pastor of his church say? What would anyone say? What does it matter what they say! I quickly told the poor man I believed he was having trouble with demons. Being desperate, he asked what he could do. Remembering the session of two nights before, I felt I was ready for anything.

"There is one thing we can do," I said. "We can cast them out."

"When?" he asked.

"Tonight," I replied, full of faith and the joy of the Lord! I was learning the meaning of the scripture which speaks of being in heavenly places in Christ!

My wife again came down into the basement kitchen with us. We sat on one side of the arena (so to speak) and this poor man sat on the other side with his wife. We started the same routine, singing choruses about the Blood of Jesus, for we didn't wish to have these demons attack us. There is nothing like a freshly applied Blood line; truly the demons cannot get through it. Then we gave the command.

To my astonishment, this man shot vertically into the air by one foot off his chair, and came down again with his head shaking to and fro as if he were a toy in a dog's mouth.

We redoubled our commands in the name of Jesus and commanded every foul suicide demon to come out. After one hour, many had come out moaning, coughing, vomiting and writhing. Then they started to speak.

We had read about demons who spoke to Jesus, but we had never heard of anyone in our day hearing demons speak. We know different now. We asked them how many more were left in the poor man, and they replied, "Twenty." We counted them as they came out, and paused at each fifth one and asked again. They told the truth, although they argued back and sometimes refused to answer. But our pressing commands in Jesus' name caused them to tell the truth. "Fifteen." "Ten." "Five." Finally the last one put up a twenty minute fight, but he came out, and the poor brother threw his head back and spoke in tongues, magnifying God.

He then made a pact with God; he said that if he was truly delivered, he would like to have God give him a gift of prophecy. And the next Sunday around the communion table, he brought forth a beautiful word of prophecy from a cleansed vessel.

Such deliverances are spectacular. They are exciting and exhilarating and build faith to high heights; but again we emphasize that such deliverances are in no way automatic. Whether or not you keep your deliverance is dependent on whether you maintain a very close walk with God. The apostle Paul expresses it simply by saying, "Work out your own salvation with fear and trembling" (Philippians 2:12); and again, the apostle James tells us that "faith without works is dead" (James 2:26).

We have known of cases where people have been delivered in a most spectacular manner, and then have returned to their old ways and the demons have returned, usually worse than before. We have known of glorious cases of deliverance from epilepsy, with demons vomiting out, and great release experienced and no more spells. But because the persons concerned did not follow on closer to the Lord than before, the demons returned.

Sometimes we have had to minister deliverance to a person for the second time, because of the re-entry of the demons. We must realize, in the first

41

place, that such demons entered into that life only because of a previous weakness; and unless that gap is closed after deliverance, the same trouble will come upon the person again. Did not Jesus say, "Behold, thou art made whole; sin no more lest a worse thing come unto thee" (John 5:14)? This man was an impotent man, but Jesus showed that his previous sin was the cause of his sickness. The remedy after deliverance was to sin no more. And when we realize that the scriptural definition of sin is "the transgression of the law," we are reminded that there is no room left for us to do as we please. The walk with God after deliverance is very narrow.

Too few Christians today have more than a vague idea of what is meant by "following Jesus." To them, He is a sentimental Lover with whom they can be as perverse as they feel inclined, and they think that Jesus will understand. They interpret being under grace, but not under law, as an excuse to do what pleases them, and they will not be tied to Scripture. These are likely to get sick and remain sick. "Sin no more, lest a worse thing come unto thee" needs to be the text of all deliverance churches today.

Perhaps the best scripture on this subject is the one which deals with the story of the man whose house was garnished, swept and cleansed after the evil spirit had gone out. This evil spirit was not to be so easily defeated. He wandered around and around, waiting for a convenient moment to return. Finally, the man backslid, and the demon *did* return and brought with him seven other spirits worse than himself (Matthew 12:43–45).

To say that this man was not saved is to misuse the plain meaning of words. Obviously, he was saved, delivered and cleansed in the Blood; but he chose to backslide, and consequently went back to his previous habit, and seven others as well. The frightful possibility of such a thing happening was made very real to me a number of years ago.

The telephone rang. "Is that you, Pastor Whyte?" It was the same man who had been delivered from 20 demons in our church kitchen seven years before.

"Yes," I replied. "What can I do for you?"

"Are you in the same place?"

"Yes."

"Do you still have the same ministry?"

"Yes."

He sighed with relief, saying he believed that God had told him to call me. He said he was down in the pit of sin again. "Do you think there's any hope for me?" he asked. "I'm in a terrible mess."

I assured him that there was indeed hope, for the mercy of God is past finding out. So he came to my office.

His story was very sordid, but a warning to us all. After his spectacular deliverance seven years before, he had moved out of the area into the suburbs, and had there attended a church which was not Full Gospel and knew nothing of healing or deliverance. It was his custom to drive downtown to his business in Toronto; and one rainy day he noticed a man at a bus stop. With compassion, he invited the man to get into his car. The man, a worldly man, offered our friend a cigarette —a friendly act, but hardly acceptable for a Full Gospel Christian. It was a wonderful opportunity for him to witness about Jesus who saves and delivers. But no. Instead, he took the cigarette, which proved to be his first step to hell on earth.

Each day, he picked up his friend and each day they smoked. And then the subject of drinking together was brought up, and so they would stop at a tavern. Then the next step was joining together in betting on the horse races. Finally the new found friend said to our brother, "I love you."

As I sat there listening to this man's story, I could hardly believe it. He had a beautiful wife, four wonderful children and a good home. I had often visited them. What power was this that drove a good Christian man to become a homosexual, leave his wife and family and live in one room with another man? Psychology cannot explain this. It was the devil working through indwelling demons.

Theology explains that no Christian can have a demon. But I remembered how God had delivered this dear brother from a suicide demon seven years before. How could this Spirit-filled man have gotten a suicide demon in the first place? And what about the demons that were in him now? I knew there was only one answer. He had come to this miserable state by disobeying the words of Scripture, "Give no place to the devil." He had allowed the devil to occupy territory which had previously been occupied by the gentle Holy Spirit.

The poor man then slumped into a chair after his terrible confession. He had scraped the bottom of the barrel of sin, but was ready to be rescued again.

Without further ado, the command was given. "Come out, in the name of Jesus." The man was ready. The filthy demons began to pour out of him with almost continual coughing and choking. Without any asking on my part, they willingly named themselves, as they came out. Lust, filth, uncleanness, perversion, cursing, etc. In twenty minutes he was completely free a second time.

When it was all over, I realized that I had seen a fulfillment of Jesus' words in Matthew 12:43–45:

"When the unclean spirit is gone out of a man, he walketh through dry places, seeking rest, and findeth none. Then he saith, I will return into my house from whence I came out; and when he is come, he findeth it empty, swept, and garnished. Then goeth he, and taketh with himself seven

*other spirits more wicked than himself, and they
enter in and dwell there: and the last state of that
man is worse than the first."*

This was the explanation of what had happened
to the man. After his first deliverance, his "house"
had been cleansed, garnished and swept clean. But
he had not kept it filled with the new Visitor, the
Holy Spirit. It had been left empty, so the suicide
spirit came back. But he also beckoned to seven
of his filthy friends, and they came in also. What
a mess a Christian can get himself into by backsliding! But thank God, there is deliverance for
all who will bend the knee to Jesus and ask Him
to forgive their sins and enter into their "houses."

Another seven years went by, and one evening
I met this brother again in a certain church. Immediately I inquired how he was doing. With joy,
he told me that after his second deliverance, he had
returned home and made a full confession to his
wife and family. They forgave him and took him
back. God then began to prosper his business and
he bought a better home. Now he was keeping his
house clean with the Blood of Jesus, and the
demon had permanently left.

We underestimate the power of demon forces;
and the very demons themselves see to it that we
are kept in ignorance, for we are not taught in
our churches about these things. No matter how
glorious your past experience has been, no matter

how often you have spoken in tongues and prophesied, no matter how exemplary your life has been in the past, you can still backslide and permit a demon to come in with seven others. The gifts of the Spirit are gifts of God, but they will not prevent you from letting in other spirits.

We have already said that speaking in tongues is not absolute proof of the baptism of the Spirit, for a demon-possessed person can speak in tongues. In the deliverance of a demon possessed girl in the Philippines in 1955, through the ministry of Reverend Lester Sumrall, the demon spoke perfect English through an ignorant girl of seventeen, who could not speak her own Philippine dialect properly. When the demon was cast out, the girl could not speak in English anymore. It is hard for us to believe that tongues once spoken by the Spirit of God could finally end up being tongues spoken by a demon power that has taken over, because of grievous backsliding in our own lives. Living close to God is the only answer.

Once we have opened our lives to the spirit world, we must be careful that only the Holy Spirit possesses us, and that we are kept under the precious Blood of Jesus. No demon can get through the Blood line. In my own experience, when delivering a man, I have heard the demon actually sing and prophesy before being cast out. In such cases, the face of the person is usually contorted in horrible shapes, but the utterances can deceive.

Be wise! You can backslide into Satan's waiting grasp even though you speak in tongues.

We would like to state as plainly as possible that, though God is restoring his power to the church to drive out demons, the suffering person, whether a Christian or unbeliever, *must be willing to be delivered.* We have found, in the case of moral perverts, alcoholics and drug addicts, that though they say with their lips that they want deliverance, yet deep down in their hearts they want temporary respite only, and not real deliverance to serve a living God. They are ashamed but unrepentant. Let me warn you that these *cannot be delivered* even if we spend hours with them. A great deal of searching questions and other operations of the gift of discerning of spirits will be necessary.

This ministry does not rest on sentimentality. We may feel sympathetic for people, but unless they are willing, they cannot be helped. Even if we were to cast the devil out of them (which is possible), he would only go back into them again as soon as our back was turned. Not only must the person be willing to be delivered, but also to *stay delivered.* The hole in the hedge that let Satan in must be closed after he has been cast out. The person must stop fearing and live close to God.

In this respect, we learned a lesson early. A Christian lady (so called) was in a real tantrum one day, and was rebuking me severely. But I determined that I was not going to be rebuked by a backslidden lady! I therefore commanded the demon to come out of her. It did (at least one of them did) and caught me by the throat and started to strangle me. I cried, "The Blood!" three times, and it went back into her. But while it had been trying to throttle me, the demon in the lady said, "There you are, *you* have a demon!" But it was a lie of Satan. And, through the Blood, I overcame the demon.

On another occasion I was asleep. In the middle of the night, I awoke to realize that the life had nearly been choked out of me. My heart was strongly oppressed. I felt as if life was almost gone. I cried, "The Blood!" three times. The demon departed rapidly, and the rest of the night was spent in peace. The next night at the same time, the same experience happened to my wife, and the same usage of the Blood brought instant deliverance. No demon can get through the Blood, but it has to be in place by faith.

I realize that these experiences may scare the timid soul from entering fully into his inheritance. But I would like to remind you that Jesus' promise still stands: "Behold, I give unto you power to tread on serpents and scorpions, and over all the power of the enemy, and nothing shall by any means hurt you" (Luke 10:19). Satan's great weapon is fear. We must refuse to fear; we must be bold in the strength of our Savior, who has told us to fear nothing. There is nothing to fear. Satan is a defeated foe. Remember that some demons said long ago, "Jesus I know, and Paul I know, but who are you?" (Acts 19:15), showing that demons will recognize the man of God as bearing the same authority as Jesus, if he exercises the power and authority that Jesus has given him.

In Acts 1:8 we read that power is to come upon us when the Holy Spirit comes in. Many people today are looking in vain for a demonstration of the power of God. No car goes forward until it is put into gear. In like manner, no Holy Ghost filled Christian will produce any power until faith is exercised, and until it is determined in our hearts that we (in Christ) are going to put an end to this evil thing right now. It is the Christian who takes action who gets results. The praying Christian on his knees can attack the devil's stronghold with great effect. "Every place that the sole of your foot shall tread upon, that have I given unto you . . ." (Joshua 1:3). We must place our foot on Satan's neck, and take him by the tail and cast him out.

CHAPTER 5

THE PERSONALITY OF DEMONS

Demons have distinct and unique personalities, just as human beings do. No two demons are the same. I have seen some highly unusual demonic personalities manifesting themselves through people.

I remember one Watch Night service. The night was cold—it was near zero outside—and as the people came into the heated church, they began to cough, and this coughing persisted, and made preaching difficult.

Suddenly the Holy Spirit showed me that this was a demon sent in to worry the preacher and disturb the meeting. I stopped and asked everyone to stand who had coughed, was coughing or intended to cough. About fifteen persons stood, looking surprised. A sound rebuke was given in the name of Jesus to this disturbing spirit, and believe it or not, no one coughed for the rest of that meeting! What wonderful things we can do if we exercise our authority as sons of God; but the devil fools us!

It is important to remember that neither Satan nor his demon spirits are "things." Neither can they be taken lightly. Demons are *beings* having malign intelligence, and each one desires to find a body wherein to express himself. A demon is not happy unless he has a body, for he does not possess a physical body himself, and so he seeks those of humans or animals.

Many of our sicknesses which seem to be mere physical problems are actually caused by demons, and should be treated as such. For instance, Jesus rebuked a spirit of fever in Peter's wife's mother. But if this fever was only a physical problem, then how foolish to rebuke it! It makes no sense whatsoever to rebuke an inanimate "thing." One can only rebuke something having intelligence, and Jesus knew that this fever was caused by a spirit. And so the spirit of fever left the lady, because it had to obey the voice of Jesus.

The following is a list of evil spirits, demons or devils, taken from the scriptures. Each one is a personality, and the word used expresses their nature: Spirit of infirmity or weakness, deaf spirit, dumb spirit, blind spirit, foul spirit, unclean spirit,

spirit of divination, spirit of bondage, spirit of error, spirit of false doctrines, seducing spirits, jealous spirit, lying spirit, familiar spirit, spirit of anti-christ, spirit of fear, perverse spirit, sorrowful spirit, spirit of slumber, spirit of whoredoms, and destroying spirit.

Satan, their undisputed overlord, has absolute dictatorial sway over them, and his names are as follows, also showing his variable characteristics: Lucifer, Prince of the power of the air and of this world, Prince of devils or demons, the Destroyer, Angel of Light, the Old Serpent, the Great Dragon, the Devil, Leviathan, Father of Lies, Murderer (and he called himself God!). Is it any wonder that we are continually afflicted, frustrated, oppressed, perplexed, worried, and tormented by these things? They swarm around us like mosquitoes in northern Canada, and once we are filled with the Holy Spirit we become target No. 1 for their evil intentions.

The most common form of attack is *oppression*. Oppression is a spiritual "pressing down," which develops a condition called "mental depression." If this condition is tolerated, then something worse may develop. For instance, if an idea which is contrary to the Word of God is entertained for too long, we become *obsessed* by that wrong idea or doctrine. Many false prophets today are demon obsessed. Then, the final state of either of these (if we willingly persist) is *possession*. Here again, though, we need to differentiate between possession of a part of the body, as in epilepsy, and possession of the soul which will lead to eternal separation from God. It is entirely possible for a Christian to end up in this latter kind of possession. No sin can be forgiven unless it is confessed with the heart and covered by the Blood of Jesus. If a Christian persists in sin, if he turns back to the things that he once enjoyed, then the Bible says there is no more sacrifice for sins, but a "certain fearful looking for of judgment and fiery indignation" (Hebrews 10:27). And nothing will change that unless this willful disobedience is confessed and put under the Blood.

Many have been so disobedient for so many years that Satan has them in the power of his demons. In many cases, these need to be delivered by their Pastors. I believe that all trouble in local churches is caused by unspiritual members who give way to Satan's demons. Probably, such people are only oppressed, but it is a dangerous state in which to persist. A church split is always the work of a grinning demon. Jesus preached love and unity.

The following experiment was carried out some years ago on our two eldest boys who were quarreling. We rebuked this disturbing spirit and commanded it to cease from troubling them. The boys instantly were released and stopped their disputing.

On another occasion, one of our members had a store, and over this store was a fine apartment which rented at $125.00 a month. The owner was distressed because she could not rent it, and had thereby lost $1,100.00. The Lord showed us that this was again the work of Satan to withhold money, to disturb, frustrate and impoverish. We agreed to go next week to the store and apartment. We went up into the apartment with the owner, and together agreed for this restraining, evil power to leave. We pleaded the Blood of Jesus in every room and cupboard, and commanded the evil spirit to leave. Then a word of prophecy was given to the effect that the apartment would be rented within a week. Within two days it was rented.

The evil presence which had been cast out then descended into the store below, and business started falling off for no reason whatsoever. Adjustments were made in certain price levels, but it created no more business. There were staff troubles, disputes and unpleasantness. The demon had gone downstairs. Special prayer was made, but it took several months for that malign spirit to finally leave. Now both the apartment and the business are flourishing!

Another unique demon personality was encountered when I was ministering in Caxton Hall, Westminster, London, England, when an insane girl walked in to be prayed for. She was one of many awaiting ministry, and when her turn came, the friend who brought her explained that she had been brought out of a mental home in order to come to this meeting.

I did not inquire as to the type of insanity, but laid my hands on the woman's head and started to rebuke the demon spirits. But nothing happened. As I looked at her, I noticed that her face had the strained look of one in torment. The Spirit of God, through the gift of the word of knowledge, showed me that her trouble was due to a persecution complex, and that she thought that everyone was against her and gossiping about her. When I faced her with this revelation, she admitted that it was true.

I then explained to her that this was a sin, and that she must confess this sin to God and ask His forgiveness before she could expect to be delivered. She seemed quite surprised, but agreed, and prayed with me before the assembly, asking God to forgive her for thinking such stupid thoughts.

I then laid my hands on her head again and prayed, and the spirit of insanity immediately left, and her face began to radiate with a bright smile of understanding and joy. I told her to turn around and face the congregation. It turned out to be a great time of rejoicing, as she praised the Lord for His healing power.

I learned an important principle from this case. Before we pray for many to be delivered, it may first be necessary for them to pray for forgiveness for themselves. Confession must first be made unto salvation. Jesus cannot forgive us anything, or de-

liver us until we say we are sorry. How hard this
is for some!

I made another discovery about another demon
personality in Bogota, Colombia, South America,
where I was ministering for Reverend Bob Lazear
of the Presbyterian Church. A Colombian pastor
had asked me to go to the city hospital to pray for
a lady who was dying. The Lutheran pastor drove
me to the hospital, and when we entered the hospital room, we saw a pathetic sight.

The woman was unconscious, and a rubber tube
was inserted into her windpipe. She was drawing
oxygen from a bottle, and her nose and mouth were
taped shut. Her relatives had not left the room for
four days. Hour by hour, they had stayed there
weeping, which was not a good atmosphere of
faith. The doctors informed me that she had but
two hours to live.

I had been called to help, but what could I
do? I hadn't the faintest idea, but I knelt by the bed
and asked God to help me. As I did so, I felt a
strange peace descend into that room, and all the
relatives likewise felt it. It was the Spirit of God
descending upon us. I took the young lady's hand,
and laid my other hand on her forehead, and said,
"Death, I rebuke you in Jesus' name." I left the
hospital, and the next day was informed that the
young lady had rapidly regained consciousness.
Within one week she was released from the hospital.

The Colombian pastor was astonished, and asked

me to come into his office. He informed me that he felt ashamed of his Presbyterian church, and that no one had been able to do this.

"Yes," I said, "but it was Jesus who healed her, not me."

"Yes," he replied, "but you *rebuked death*. I've never heard anyone do that before."

I simply replied that Jesus probably would have done the same if in my position, for death is a spirit. This healing had a great effect on the Presbyterian church in Colombia, and they began to be open to the working of the Holy Spirit among them.

Some of the demons I have met are so extraordinary that I have hesitated to put the stories into print. The "music demon" is a case in point.

I was staying with friends in Dunedin, Florida, and was visiting the wife of a member of the Full Gospel Businessmen's Fellowship. I asked her to explain her trouble.

She said that everywhere she went, her head was filled with music, so that it was almost impossible at times to concentrate on what she was doing. I must frankly confess that this rather amused me, and I asked her what was wrong with a built-in radio playing all the time, and was it classical music or rock and roll?

"No," she said, "it's not rock and roll, it's good music."

This was indeed a puzzle. If it had been rock and roll, I might have quickly said that the devil was behind this. But good music? What should I say?

Then she looked me squarely in the face and said, "You are a man of God. Tell me, is it a demon?"

I was on the spot! This is one of those cases where you quickly say, "Lord, show me! Lord, help me!" And as soon as I inquired of the Lord, the reply came back loud and clear into my mind.

"Yes," the Holy Spirit said, "this *is* a demon."

So I told the lady that it *was* a demon, but at this point I had no idea of its name. So we began to pray together, and the Lord revealed to me that this was a *distracting demon*. As soon as this spirit was commanded to come out in Jesus' name, it did so by coughing out, a most common form of ejection. After about one minute, she was delivered of a distracting music spirit, and has remained free since that day.

Another demon personality was encountered in Dallas, Texas, at the Bible School of Christ for the Nations. A certain woman came for prayer, and as usual, I asked, "What do you want from Jesus?" She replied that she was afraid of destroying herself and her three children. Satan's intention was to wipe out the whole family. I then began to bind and command these murder demons to leave. I was not surprised when she began to scream in a loud voice, for I knew that Jesus had encountered this kind of demonic reaction many times (see Luke 4:33). It was not a pleasant experience. The demons manifested themselves in a frenzy of rage and then started to vomit out.

These murder demons were somewhat stronger than most of the demons with which we deal. I have learned that strong demons usually vomit out, often bringing mucus with them and sometimes even the poison that surrounds them. This is quite an operation! The very hand of Jesus, the Divine Physician, reaches right inside them and brings salvation and healing. I have seen many expensive operations done by Jesus for free, and the results are often left on the floor or in buckets. Gruesome and horrible, but true.

Read on, gentle reader.

This deliverance took about half an hour. Then, as is usual in such cases, we began to pray for her to be baptized in the Holy Spirit. We taught her to plead the Blood of Jesus out loud. While she was praying that prayer, Jesus gave her a new tongue and she began to speak as the Spirit gave utterance. The vessel that had been filled with murder was now filled with love. What a transformation! The name of Jesus can cast out every foul spirit, and the applied Blood of Jesus can cleanse the vessel. This opens the way for the Holy Spirit to come in and do his work.

These experiences taught me many lessons. We must not stop wrestling. We must never stop fighting. So many people are prayed for and because they do not get instant relief, they quit resisting.

There should never be a moment when you quit resisting the devil. We can cast him out of our lives, our homes, our offices and factories. We are sons of God. We have been given dominion over every creature, including demons. We have dominion in the name of the Lord.

A brother minister told me the following story which took place in the Spring of 1957. He had gone down to the Bahama Islands to preach in a church. No pastor had ever been able to stay there, because the unfriendly natives would come out from the bush beating their drums and shouting obscenities and making worship impossible.

Our friend accepted the challenge. The first thing he did was to walk around the outside of the church property, pleading the Blood of Jesus aloud, for Satan to hear and God to honor. Once was enough. Now there is peace. The disturbing evil spirit has departed. A new missionary is to take over the church, and God's work will go on.

It is my belief that we do not speak enough of the Blood of Jesus in our worship, our praying and our attacks on Satan's strongholds. I am sure that if Christian assemblies everywhere would magnify the Blood of Jesus, we would see carnal members stirred up and much blessing outpoured in new life for the church.

CHAPTER 6

THE CASTING OUT OF DEMONS

It was in Brooklyn, New York, on a Sunday morning. I was ministering in a Full Gospel Church. The pastor and his wife were recent graduates of a Bible School in Lima, New York. He was leading a group song service, when suddenly a woman in the congregation was seen to begin swaying from side to side, with a look of contortion and agony spread across her face. She started to bump into those on either side of her, and it was obvious to me that she was in torment.

Turning to the pastor, I said, "Do you see that woman down there? You are seeing a first-class case of a religious demon operating."

He was startled. "What shall we do?"

It was then that I had to rely on the gifts of the

Spirit. The Lord told me to go down and speak to the woman. However, at that point, I did not know what God would have me say to her. But I told the pastor to carry on leading the singing, and I went to the woman and said, "Sister, you are tormented."

"Yes," she replied, "I know."

Then I explained that I would pray for her after the service along with the others, and told her to sit down and behave in the name of the Lord, which she did.

At the end of the service my wife and I approached the lady and asked her if she was willing for us to pray for her. She replied that she was, so I began to rebuke the religious demon in Jesus' name. Immediately, it started to scream with that unearthly sound that comes in such cases. I had to go around the church, closing every window because it was summertime, and the people were astonished at what was happening. By the time I returned from this chore, my wife had her hands on the woman's shoulders, and was holding her from being hurled to the floor, so great was the agitation of the demons. After about ten minutes of screaming and violent coughing spells, she was delivered, and then said, "Why hasn't anyone ever done this for me before?" What a pathetic question—and yet how appropriate. Why?

The ministry of casting out demons, or evil spirits, is one which has long been neglected by the

Christian church, probably owing to fear of the unknown. It is, however, a ministry which is coming more and more into prominence in this latter day revival.

Many people have little idea even of what a demon is, or what it can do. Most of us are familiar with the work of angels as ministering spirits to those who are the heirs of salvation (Hebrews 1:14; Psalms 91:11), but we are apt to forget that there are "evil angels" also—those who fell from their previous high estate as the trusted servants of Jehovah and were cast out of heaven with Lucifer, the son of the morning, or Satan himself. "And the great dragon was cast out, that old serpent, called the Devil and Satan, which deceiveth the whole world; he was cast out into the earth, and *his angels were cast out with him*" (Revelation 12:9).

The Bible also teaches that the Lord uses these fallen angels to visit suffering upon those who are deliberately disobedient, as in Psalm 78:49: "He cast upon them the fierceness of His anger, wrath and indignation, and trouble *by sending evil angels among them.*" We are also told in the next verse that these evil angels caused pestilence which brought death. These fallen angels are reserved under darkness awaiting the great judgment day and the coming of the Lord Jesus Christ, when they will assuredly be put down into the pit and bound with Satan for 1,000 years (Jude 6 and Revelation 20:2,3).

When Satan was cast out of heaven with his legions, he was given authority over all mankind and all the earthly creation of animals, birds, fishes and vegetation. In fact, he is able to 'influence everything that has life. And he has a very definite effect on the very atmosphere that surrounds the earth (John 12:31; 14:30; 16:11; Ephesians 2:2).

This beautiful, created being was at one time called Lucifer, which means "Shining One" (Isaiah 14:12). He held the greatest position among the created angelic hosts, but owing to pride, tried to usurp the throne which by right belonged to Jesus Christ. We must therefore remember that he did not lose his power or authority when he was cast out of heaven, but by Divine permission, uses it today among the earthly creation. His power, therefore, is second only to Jesus Christ, and is infinitely greater than many people imagine.

Obviously, though, the devil is not omnipresent nor omniscient. His power is limited. In order to carry on his great work of destruction, or more accurately, his work of maintaining the conditions of curse upon the world, he uses the innumerable company of wicked spirits, or fallen angels, to do his bidding. Without doubt these wicked spirits are governed by well disciplined angelic orders of generals and captains.

The only way we can keep safe from these terrible powers is by constantly keeping ourselves covered by faith in the Blood of Jesus, which speaks defeat to these demon spirits. This enables us to be in the blessed position described by the Psalmist as "dwelling in the secret place of the Most High and abiding under His shadow" (Psalm 91:1). There is absolutely no other protection or "shadow" than the covering of the Precious Blood of Jesus Christ.

It is not possible for us to know the number of these wicked spirits. There seems little doubt that they are far more numerous than mankind. The poor demoniac of Gadara had a legion in him. We read in Smith's Standard Bible Dictionary that a legion consists of about 6,000 men and is used in the Bible to express any large number, with the accessory ideas of order and subordination (Matthew 24:53; Mark 5:9).

There seems little doubt that every accident, misfortune, quarrel, sickness, disease, and unhappiness is the *direct* result of the individual work of one or more wicked spirits. These spirits are just as much *beings* as we humans, except that they have no physical form. This is why they seek to indwell humans or animals (as in the case of the swine into which the Lord cast the legion from the demoniac of Gadara). They may even seek to re-enter a body when the spirit of that person ceases to resist their forces (Matthew 12:43–45).

They can shrink to the size of a pin head or enlarge so that one demon can fill the whole being of a man. In the latter case, we say that a person is "demon possessed," i.e., entirely under the control of an evil, spiritual being who has gained possession.

That Jesus meant us to resist is obvious from the writings of the Apostle James. "Resist the devil," he says, "and he will flee from you" (James 4:7). To resist means to be on guard, knowingly covered with His Blood, and keeping ourselves under control. A drunken man is wide open to demon possession because of his lack of control. One who loses his temper is also similarly exposed. Unregenerate sick people who are weakened by suffering are also exposed unless someone prays for them by faith. And again, anyone who has anything to do with spiritism, occult sciences or bloodless cults is almost certain to be affected.

It can therefore be seen that the more a nation departs from God and His love as shown in Jesus Christ, the more does that nation become controlled by demonic powers. So also with individuals. Paul made this clear when he wrote, "For we wrestle not against flesh and blood, but against principalities, against powers, against the rulers of the darkness of this world, against wicked spirits in heavenly places" (Ephesians 6:12, margin). These demon powers control the rulers of darkness and live in the first heaven of the earth's atmosphere. They do not live in heaven, for it was from there they were ejected.

The Apostle Paul shows what sort of armor we

need to resist and fight them (Ephesians 6:13–18); and conversely, if we do not follow his advice, then we are exposed to demon powers and we must not blame God, for we have been warned.

Of course I do not want to fail to mention that God's angels play their part in protecting us, for Gabriel was opposed by Satan in coming to help Daniel after his three weeks of fasting and prayer. And it was not until Michael came and helped that the victory was won over the demon powers who were opposing (Daniel 10:13). Both Gabriel and Michael had their own armies fighting in this battle. In Psalm 91:11 we are informed that good angels protect us from the small mishaps of life which are directly caused by demon spirits. Is it not wonderful to think that God's children, by faith in Jesus Christ, are the object of angelic care?

Where evil spirits gain entrance into a person's body, we speak of *demon oppression*, for these demons use the body of the poor unfortunate person to work their wicked acts, and actually control them and speak through them. At other times, evil spirits will take control of a person's mind, and this is called *demon obsession*. One of the greatest evidences of this is the delusion of the sufferer in thinking that he has committed the unpardonable sin. However, on questioning him he is unable to tell you what constitutes the unpardonable sin!

Demons can swarm around a person and worry, tempt and distract him. This would be another example of *demon oppression*. They might cause us to get "out of victory," or lose our temper, a condition in which no Christian need ever be. Many afflictions from which we suffer are caused by demons. Consider the spirits which are described in the scriptures as foul, wicked, evil, deaf, dumb, infirm, unclean, seducing, etc. Many of our infirmities are caused by minute demons working their irritation and destruction in our very bones and muscles.

Many believe that a cancer is nothing more than a work of evil spirits which, when cast out in the mighty Name of Jesus, shrivels up and dies. Who would dispute the possibility that arthritis, tumors, deafness, dumbness, etc., may not be the actual work of demons in portions of the body? We do not say that such a person is "demon possessed," but we do suggest that they are sorely afflicted by demons.

One day a lady came into our church in Toronto. She had heard our radio broadcast, and was fascinated about the healing that God was doing in our midst. She was suffering from degeneration of the spine, which would lead ultimately to a life in a wheel chair. She was a great swimmer and gave swimming lessons, and was greatly concerned about the outcome of her life. So I took dominion over the destroying spirit of infirmity which was working in her spine, and immediately she received healing.

Quite understandably, this miracle of healing completely changed her whole understanding of New Testament Christianity. She had a daughter, Gail, who had severely injured her ankle doing gymnastics at school. She had been taking cortisone for some months to kill the pain. But it wasn't getting any better.

So one day, Gail came to church, limping, and carrying a cane. At the end of the service when everyone else had gone, she remained behind with her mother and shyly asked for prayer. Naturally, I agreed but was greatly surprised when she asked, "Can I do a hand spin after prayer?"

"Cartwheels in church?" I asked, laughing. "Why not, if Jesus is in the act!"

Hands were laid on Gail and prayer was made, and then without further ado, she turned on her hands and feet *in church*, proving that Jesus had healed her. That experience completely changed her whole life, and she and her mother soon received the baptism in the Holy Spirit. Later on she was delivered from other emotional problems, and finally married my son Stephen who helps in this ministry. Gail graduated from the University of Toronto with a Physical Education degree.

What a story! From my radio broadcast to a bride for my son. We never know what the Lord has in store for those that love Him.

We know that medical science teaches us that the cause of much sickness is germs, i.e., small parasitic creatures of minute size which breed in a portion of the body, multiply and cause great distress; but there are other sicknesses which do not appear to be caused by germs. We may well ask ourselves if God does not have some way of protecting his people from these germs. God is omnipotent, and nothing is beyond His power. Certainly, He can send His ministering spirits to protect us and to prevent evil spirits from putting the germs (or spores) into our bodies, if we pray for protection and keep God's laws.

Remember that nothing happens by "chance" or luck, but all is ordered by God. Demons are merely agents in the hands of Satan to do his work at his bidding in the same way that soldiers obey their officers.

Germs are part of the curse which will be destroyed at the coming of Jesus Christ, for the sevenfold increase of light from the sun will destroy all germ-life during the Millenium (Isaiah 30:26). In our experience we have positively proved this fact. When boiling water has been spilt on human flesh, immediate "pleading of the Blood" over such an injured person has prevented inflammation, showing clearly that it is the demons which visit the germs on the injured part of the body.

So with cuts or scratches. We recently rebuked the flow of blood from a deep scratch in a child's forehead, and it immediately stopped. The wound was pinched together and the next day the child

71

was running around as if nothing had happened. The finest disinfectant in the world is the Blood of Jesus Christ, applied by faith, for it keeps all unclean spirits away, if used in faith.

The summation of all this, we believe, is that the primary cause of all sickness is spiritual; and although symptoms may be treated by natural means, yet if the power of the Name of Jesus Christ is invoked, and His shed Blood used as a weapon against Satan in faith, then certainly we will see Divine healing in manifestation, because the cause of the sickness is destroyed at the root.

That Jesus meant us to differentiate between divine healing and exorcism of demons, however, is apparent in His last discourse to His disciples. He taught them to expect *five* signs as proving the ministry of the Word of God (Mark 16:17–18). The first of these five signs was the casting out of devils in His name. It is interesting that this particular sign should be mentioned before the sign of physical healing. We do not know whether this order is accidental, but we suspect that Jesus had a reason for putting demon deliverance first, because He always dealt with primary things first. If we would first cast out demons, we would frequently have no need to pray for the sick; deliverance from the demon would bring all the healing needed.

However, we must remember that this is a ministry of faith. In Acts 19:13 we read of the disastrous results that followed when experimenting, unbelieving Jews tried to cast out demons by using the Name of Jesus without faith. The demons reacted, and showed their great power by tearing the clothes off the seven sons of Sceva.

To confirm our thought that casting out of demons is of more primary importance than laying on of hands for healing, it is interesting to note that the very first recorded act by Jesus in bringing deliverance was to cast out a devil. We read about this in Mark 1:24–26, where Jesus rebuked an evil, unclean spirit, and it obeyed and came out of the poor man, rending him and using the man's mouth to "cry with a loud voice." If this ministry was so important to Jesus, should it be any less important to us?

CHAPTER 7

UNDERSTANDING YOUR AUTHORITY

The Apostle James tells us that the devils believe and tremble at the Name of Jesus. This should help us to understand that we have great authority over these demons. We can afford to deal with them as defeated foes.

I once had a spectacular experience which helped me to realize this fact. I was talking to a brother minister in our sanctuary. Suddenly, a drunk man lurched into the church and started to insult us. Realizing that I was face to face with a demon, I rebuked it in Jesus' name and commanded it to be subject to me. The results were extraordinary.

The man started to jump up and down and curse the name of Jesus. Then he pulled off his jacket and threw it into the air. All the time, I was binding and rebuking Satan. Then he tore off his shirt and threw it away, and put his hands into his pockets and pulled out all his money and threw the coins all over the church.

He then came forward to where we were sitting and began arguing that he knew more about "religion" than we did. I continued to rebuke and bind the demons. Finally he fell to the floor and started to spin around and around like a top. The demons were completely under our control, and it was a very interesting experience to be taking dominion over the devil this way.

Suddenly the man stopped spinning, got to his feet, started back to where his shirt was lying, put it on, and began to pick up his scattered coins. I helped him retrieve as many as I could. Then, after I had helped him on with his jacket, he sauntered out of the church very peacefully.

It was a dramatic demonstration of the power we have over demons. I knew that I would never again need to be afraid of anything or anybody. It was good to know of our practical protection against the powers of darkness, which are continually arrayed against us.

This power over demons was again demonstrated when I encountered a spirit of insanity. The girl who was oppressed by this spirit was named Mary. She had been incarcerated in Whitby Mental Hospital in Ontario. However, for a period each month, she would return to sanity. But with the approach of her menstrual cycle, she would become violently insane.

Sometimes, her mother, who was a Christian Scientist, was able to take her from the hospital for a few days during her safe period, but was warned to get her back to the hospital well before the next seizure.

One day the mother heard about our ministry of casting out demons, and so she approached me to see if I could help. As a Christian Scientist, she knew nothing whatsoever of the ministry of exorcism. She had been taught that her daughter was not really sick, and that it was "all in her mind."

It was arranged that Mary should be brought to the church office by her mother during her safe period. However, she had apparently waited a little too long, for on the way to the church, the mother realized that she was in a very dangerous predicament. Her daughter was losing her mind!

As soon as Mary got out of the car, she started shouting, "I'm not going in there!" Efforts were made to calm her, but to no effect. She turned and ran away into the Bloor Street traffic. Naturally, the mother was extremely disturbed, but I assured her in faith that we could take dominion over this demon and command Mary to return. We did not phone the police; we "phoned" Jesus instead. And sure enough, in ten minutes, Mary returned. But she still insisted that she was not going to enter the church.

"Mary," I said in a stern voice, "I command you in the name of Jesus to go inside." And immediately she obeyed.

Once we were inside, I commanded her to enter the office. And again I commanded her to sit down. She was very obedient to every command. I was learning in a practical way that we do indeed have power over the enemy.

Her mother explained to me that at times Mary would get very violent and try to push her hands through glass windows. It was as well that I was warned. I began to command these insane demons to come out of her. It was a long battle, possibly because the mother was present and was not exercising real faith. After about an hour, Mary uttered some terrible screams, as some demons came out of her. At that point though, other demons in her became greatly agitated and she started to her feet, intending to push her hands through the glass windows. I remembered that if one punched a person in the solar plexus and temporarily winded them, this would stop such an action. So I gave her a sharp dig in this area, and she immediately collapsed back again into a sitting position, and more screams occurred. I am not recommending this as normal treatment in such a case, nor defending my actions, but in this case it worked.

She calmed down somewhat, but was obviously out of her mind and still greatly agitated. It was now about 2:00 a.m. on Sunday morning, and we decided to take her back to the mental hospital.

"He'll never arrive," she growled. "I'll jab my cigarette in his neck while he is driving."

As we started, I again rebuked the spirits and commanded them to be silent. Very shortly she went to sleep beside her mother in the back seat. My wife was riding with me in the front seat and praying continually. Soon, we had her safely back in the hospital.

The next day, she had the worst spell of raging insanity she had ever had, and had to be put into a special room which was padded. Interestingly enough, after this attack, she never had another one. The demons had yielded to our authority. The last we saw of Mary some years later, she was acting as a counselor in a Billy Graham Crusade.

I was not surprised at this manifestation of dominion over demons. The Bible teaches us that Jesus gave his power to the twelve apostles (Matthew 10:8), and later to the seventy, for when they returned from their first missionary journey, they exclaimed with joy, "Even the devils are subject unto us *through thy name*." Then He gave them a wonderful promise, and this promise is also for us today: "Behold, I give unto you power to tread on scorpions, and over all the power of the enemy: *and nothing shall by any means hurt you*" (Luke 10:17–19). We are therefore assured that we can go forward and cast out demons in His name, and they will not hurt us, for He has given us complete *power* or *authority* over all the power of the devil.

Another example of this power over demons concerns my eldest son, David, who married a fine Christian girl named Genevieve from Northern Ireland. Her mother was suffering from bursitis and ever-worsening arthritis in her right arm. She had been unable to raise her arm for three years. She knew nothing of divine deliverance, but Genevieve asked me to call on her and pray for her. So when I arrived, I found a kind Irish lady who was unable to lift her arms very much, and whose hands were knotted and full of pain. She was able to get about only with much difficulty. It was obvious that her final state would be in a wheel chair.

I explained that the type of prayer I would pray would be different from that which she had previously known. I was not going to ask Jesus to heal her, but I would pray the way He told his disciples to pray. I also explained that in such diseases as arthritis, it is often necessary to examine one's self to see if there is any criticism, grumblings or self pity. If these are recognized, they must be forsaken and the forgiveness of Jesus sought. This she did.

Then she sat down, and I began to rebuke the binding spirits in Jesus' name. As I kept this up, she began to break out in sweat drops, and she looked up and said, "I've never heard anyone pray like that before!"

I continued praying this way for about ten minutes. Then feeling that a work of healing was beginning, I told her to lift her arm above her head. She found this very painful, so I gently helped her, and together, we got the arm up. But she was crying with pain and sweating profusely. It seemed like a difficult beginning, but by the time I left her home she was able to raise her arm above her head and all the pain was gone out of her hands and she was able to move them freely.

What had happened? I had cast out a spirit of bondage that was binding her joints. This happens in hundreds of cases of arthritis. Now this lady tells everyone and demonstrates her healing. Oh, the glorious liberty of the children of God! (Romans 8:21)

The deliverance ministry was very manifest in the early church after Pentecost. Philip, the evangelist, was credited with working miracles. "For unclean spirits crying with a loud voice, came out of many that were possessed with them" (Acts 8:6–7). Again, Paul was grieved with the spirit of divination in the young girl who kept crying out, "These men are the servants of the Most High God which show unto us the way of salvation" (Acts 16:16–18). Today, many would applaud such utterances as great demonstrations of discernment. But Paul knew better, and after many days he commanded the spirit of divination to come out of her, and her vile employers lost their living. The evil spirit took the best part of an hour to obey the command of Paul. But finally, they had to yield to his authority. Evil spirits even came out when handkerchiefs and aprons which had been prayed over by Paul were brought in contact with possessed persons (Acts 19:11–12).

We could enumerate other Scriptural examples, but we wish to dwell on *today*. The ministry of casting out evil spirits is a glorious reality *today*. We have witnessed many wonderful deliverances of sufferers from suicide demons, epileptic demons, arthritic demons, cancer demons, insane demons, asthma demons, foul demons, sex demons, religious demons, fear demons, jealousy demons, etc. These have frequently come out crying with a loud voice, sometimes accompanied by vomitings, spittings, coughings and writhings. They have even argued back and refused to come out, but have done so ultimately. It is impossible to classify all these cases, but they all come out at the command of faith *in the name of the Lord Jesus*. Deliverance is always certain, although it can be delayed and take a period of time. In fact, more than one period of spiritual battle may have to be entered into before final deliverance is obtained for the victim. But victory is certain.

One beautiful deliverance took place when my good friend, Dr. Russell Meade, of Chicago Bible College, one day brought a young college graduate for prayer. Dr. Meade has been used in the deliverance ministry and has written five excellent articles for *Christian Life* magazine, which were later published in book form.

This young man had a great need. It is not necessary to go into a detailed explanation, but let it be sufficient to say that he was bound by a lust spirit. Naturally, I asked him if he was married, and he replied that he was. Certainly, it would be a very unpleasant thing for a wife to have a husband bound by a lust spirit, and so I asked no more questions. I knew the name of the spirit, and that was enough. I commanded it to come out in Jesus' name. Immediately, we saw the familiar choking ejection through the throat, and after ten minutes all deliverance ceased, and it was obvious that he had been healed.

Some months later we met Dr. Meade in Chicago, and he referred to this young man. Apparently his wife had come to him and said, "Where did you take my husband?"

"To Toronto," he said, "to Brother Whyte's church."

"Well, what did you do?" She inquired.

"We prayed for him," he replied.

"Well," she said, "I don't know what you did, but I would like you to know that I have a completely changed husband." A wife should know, shouldn't she?

Thousands are bound by this lust spirit. It takes many beastly forms and is ugly and foul, causing misery to many. But this is the day of the visitation of God's love. You can be delivered.

However, willing agreement and co-operation by

the sufferer is of greatest importance. This is true with alcoholics. If they do not go on with God after the demons have been cast out, the demons will quickly come back again (Matthew 12:43–45).

Cases of pernicious anemia, asthma, high blood pressure, colitis and heart trouble have positively been healed by commanding the spirits of infirmity to leave the body, which they do with open manifestations. Some even see "dark shadows" leave them and feel a tremendous sense of relief.

To those of you who believe that the Lord Jesus Christ was anointed that He might "open the prison to them that are bound" (Isaiah 61:1), may we urge that you put into practice Jesus' wonderful promise, "In my name shall they cast out devils" (Mark 16:17). Put away timidity and uncertainty, knowing that "nothing shall by any means hurt you" (Luke 10:19). But before beginning this ministry, cover yourself by faith in the precious Blood and keep under its shadow, going into battle with the full Gospel armor. It is not necessary to shout at demons; they hear quite easily and will obey you. Your faith will rise as never before as you behold the wonderful deliverances that can be wrought today in the mighty name of Jesus.

CHAPTER 8

THE SATANIC REALITY
OF THE OCCULT

I was preaching in the auditorium of the City Hall in Hamilton, Bermuda. There was a Scottish lady present who had not previously heard the message of healing and deliverance. Apparently it took a little time to digest!

Some months later she visited our church in Toronto, and came for prayer for healing. She had arthritis. I had been informed, however, that this lady was a regular attender at a spiritist church and had no connection whatsoever with the Christian faith. But she came seeking healing.

I explained that I must be frank, and ask her if it was true that she was attending spiritist services and seances.

"Yes," she said, "and I have received so much benefit from them; I have found God in a much closer way and He has helped me so much."

I gently explained to her that all forms of the occult are expressly forbidden in the Scriptures and that God has said that all who take any part in this type of activity will actually be cut off or severed from His Presence—which was quite the opposite of her testimony about how close she was to God.

"Would you like me to show you in the Bible where all forms of spiritism are expressly forbidden by God?" I asked.

"Yes," she said, "please show me." And I opened up to Leviticus 19:31, Leviticus 20:6, and Isaiah 8:19.

This was enough. She immediately renounced all forms of occultism and necromancy, for she had had *no idea* that it was forbidden by God. She was very humble about the whole matter, and when I prayed for her, the Lord instantly healed her of all arthritis, stiffness and pain, and the healing has remained good over the years. A week after her deliverance, she returned to the church and was prayed for, and was mightily baptized in the Holy Spirit, speaking in tongues. She writes regularly from Scotland, and her faith is firm.

I read recently that every American high school has its witch or witches. (In the Bible, the male version is called a wizard, and both male and female witches are possessed of a "familiar spirit." See

Deuteronomy 18:10-12.) Spiritism is now openly practiced on every American campus. Witchcraft is rife in Britain. And in Brazil it is an epidemic. Demonism is on the increase because people are departing from God and His Word, and the vacuum thereby created in the human spirit is being filled by "other spirits." Man is "having fun" communicating with demons, and he thinks it isn't so bad. He is told that there is "white magic" and "black magic," and that there are "good spirits" and "bad spirits." The truth is that many bad spirits pretend to be good in order to deceive. All demons are bad, even if they pose as "angels of light."

One time I was faced with a beautiful young girl of about sixteen. To look at her, she seemed the type you would meet at church. But Satan is an arch deceiver. This girl first told me that she had been on drugs. Then she confessed that she had also been acting in the role of a witch at school. Apparently she had two demons.

I laid my hands upon her head and rebuked the demons and commanded them to come out in Jesus' name. Immediately they started to scream, for they realized their impotency before the name of Jesus and His shed Blood. They screamed and choked her, and this went on for a full hour, with many other Christian students entering in and helping. After lunch, she had been completely delivered, and so I asked her if she would like to be filled with the Holy Spirit. She readily agreed, and she was taught to plead and honor the Blood of Jesus in prayer. Soon the Holy Spirit entered into her, and she began to speak in a beautiful unknown tongue! I couldn't help but marvel at the wonderful change that had come over her.

I realize that this book may come as a great shock to those "that are at ease in Zion" (Amos 6:1). This is the day of deliverance, the day of unveiling of secrets long lost to a sleeping church (Matthew 25:5).

How many Christians are indeed wrestling against demon powers? How many are arrayed in their Gospel armor? Our churches have taken on the aspects of social clubs, not military barracks! We neither know our enemy, nor the arms that God gives us to fight him. We do not want to fight, we want to dream, and church splits become the fashion. Nervous breakdowns by God's servants are commonplace. Anything goes in many Full Gospel churches. Hollywood evangelism thrives, and signs and wonders take place in large meetings for which there is no scriptural warrant or foundation, and the people are delighted and deluded! How necessary is that wonderful gift of discerning of spirits!

When the demon finally left a poor young girl in the Billidad Prison in Manila, Philippine Islands, under the ministry of Rev. Lester Sumrall, black hairs were found in the hands and under the nails of the girl. These hairs were carefully examined by experts who claimed that they were not of human or known animal origin. The girl described the demon that attacked and bit her as a "hairy monster."

If these demon hairs can be materialized and kept under lock and key in the Billidad Prison, can not other signs and wonders materialize in these days before our astonished and shocked gaze? Are we to accept every supernatural happening as of the Holy Spirit? Many people attending our churches today are themselves in need of deliverance. Many are bound and possessed, and some of their peculiar mannerisms *may* be due to this cause. Not everything that happens in a Full Gospel meeting must of necessity be interpreted as of the Holy Spirit. Can we not understand that as God is stepping up His power in the deliverance ministry today, so also is Satan stepping up his lying signs and wonders also? (Matthew 24:24).

Among those who practice spiritism and the occult arts, many unquestioned signs and wonders take place. To deny this is foolishness. Things can be made to appear and disappear. But how? Levitation of inanimate objects is a reality. Articles such as vases and drinking glasses can sail across a room and be dashed in pieces against a wall. Tables can be made to walk up walls, and voices, including "other tongues," can be heard through trumpets and other means.

We remember speaking to a Jewish friend who

had been in the company of several men in New-
castle, N.S.W., Australia, one of whom practiced
these occult arts. He boastingly said he could cause
anything to appear in the room where they were
sitting. My friend immediately asked him to "materialize" a tuna fish out of the Southern Ocean. No
sooner had the wish been made known, than a great,
flapping, wet tuna fish was right in the middle of
the room. How did it get there? How do glasses
sail through the air? How are inanimate objects
caused to be levitated, defying the natural laws of
gravity? Are all these lying signs and wonders so
much "hocus pocus," or are they real?

The answer, my friends, is that *they are real,
but they are not of God.* They are brought about
through demon powers. The demons, being in-
visible, carry the glasses, support the walking tables
upon the walls, carry such things as a tuna fish out
of the sea into a room; they have laws which we do
not know and understand, and if we open our lives,
through disobedience to God's Holy Word, we
then become the servants of these same demon
powers.

In the case of the two magicians in Pharaoh's
court, Jannes and Jambres, like modern African
witch doctors, they had power, though limited.
Moses' rod turned into a serpent, and theirs ap-
peared to do so likewise. But it must be considered
as axiomatic that Satan has no power to create.
Only God can and does create by His Word. Satan

can create nothing except confusion and havoc, by taking the things of God and prostituting them to his own ends. We do not believe that Jannes and Jambres created little serpents; we believe they merely used demon powers to have them transported from the forests into Pharaoh's court. The God-created serpent of Moses then ate up the natural-born smaller serpents, showing that God is always greater than the devil and his demon powers.

Maybe you do not believe in haunted houses! But such houses do exist for a fact. However, there are many misconceptions concerning them. You may have been told that the ghosts of departed people live in such houses, but this is not true. Demons haunt houses, and can cause thumps and bangs in the middle of the night and day. These things are real, but a Christian need have no fear, because he has the name of Jesus and His shed Blood with which to expel these demon powers who are trying to imitate a departed soul of years before.

There are also many misconceptions regarding spiritist mediums. Regardless of what they claim, spiritist mediums do not communicate with those who have gone before. Instead, they communicate with demon spirits who imitate those who have died. We can easily understand the possibility of a person being inhabited by a demon for years, and on his death, this demon roams around in a disembodied state looking for another person who will not resist his efforts to gain entrance. This demon knows many intimate things which happened in the life of the departed person, and if some medium is willing to communicate with this familiar spirit, naturally the spirit can simulate the dead person and fool the assembled gullible gathering. •

Many will agree that these things happen in spiritist seances, but they are not so willing to believe that an angel of light could come into a religious meeting and deceive the people. But we have already mentioned a number of instances where this was done. We have referred to the case of the girl with the spirit of divination who started to speak as Paul and Silas were going to prayer (Acts 16:16). We have also referred to the modern case of the man in Erie, Pennsylvania, who similarly cried out in a large meeting and was delivered. We have also referred to the man in a meeting in Toronto who created a disturbance before 2,000 people. It is in such circumstances that religious demons love to "show off."

Christians must not be gullible. Just because it is possible for a person to fall down under the power of God, we are not to assume that all falling down is of God. For instance, in the case of the deliverance of the demoniac son in Mark 9:26, we read that "the spirit cried, and rent him sore, and came out of him; and he was as one dead; insomuch that many said, He is dead." Sometimes when a person who needs deliverance comes into the presence of a person who casts out demons, the demon will cast them to the ground, or cause some other physical manifestation.

I remember delivering a girl in New York State from epilepsy. Just previous to this, she had received a glorious baptism of the Spirit and had spoken in tongues. While doing so, her left arm oscillated violently, and we noticed this and inquired about it. We were informed that this was caused by "the Holy Spirit," for every time she started to praise God her left arm started to oscillate.

We pointed out that the Holy Spirit does not cause people's arms to oscillate. We were then informed that this young girl of seventeen had epilepsy, and that her parents were intending to have a brain operation performed on her when she reached the age of twenty-one. They had been told that such an operation would relieve the pressure on the left top side of the brain. In spite of this, I informed the people present that this girl needed deliverance.

For fifteen minutes we kept up a constant rebuking of Satan's power, during which time the arm started to oscillate violently; but it progressively started to decelerate in the second fifteen minutes, and after thirty minutes it ceased all movement. We then said, "Sister, we believe you are healed." She started to weep for joy, telling us that all brain pressure had gone, and later she testified in her own church of being healed by the power of God. No operation at the age of twenty-one was necessary. The demon had been cast out.

Finally, may we urge the readers of this book to be very careful to examine the many questionable doctrines which are increasing in our midst in these last days. Doctrines that throw doubt on the reality of heaven and hell and God's judgments; doctrines that tell us no one lives again until the resurrection day—these do not belong to the revelation of the Holy Spirit, whom Jesus said would guide us into all truth. Such doctrines are revealed by other spirits.

"Now the Spirit speaketh expressly, that in the latter times some shall depart from the faith, giving heed to seducing spirits, and doctrines of devils . . ." (1 Timothy 4:1). And again, "When they shall say unto you, Seek unto them that have familiar spirits and unto wizards, that peep and that mutter; should not a people seek unto their God? on behalf of the living should they seek unto the dead? To the law and to the testimony! If they speak not according to this Word, surely there is no morning for them" (Isaiah 8:19–20, R.V.).

Let us always weigh everything carefully against the written Word of God. Amen.

ABOUT THE AUTHOR

Sovereignly led by the Holy Spirit into an understanding of demonic activity and spiritual warfare, Maxwell Whyte embarked on a journey in ministry that was fraught with uncertainty and an absence of familiar landmarks.

As is so often the case with pioneers, he was misunderstood, ridiculed, and ostracized by the Christian community, even in his own city. Despite great opposition, he forged ahead in the battle against the forces of Satan, convinced that the ministry of deliverance was scripturally based and was being restored to the church in his day.

Later, he began to record his experiences, and over the next two-and-a-half decades, he authored 18 books. His first book, "The Power of the Blood", is widely destributed throughout the world, selling over 350,000 copies, and has been translated into several languages.